BRUMBACK LIBRARY

3 3045 00105 4418

D1788802

$16.45
j595.76 Hartley, Linda.
HAR   Rhinoceros
           beetle to the

CHILDREN'S DEPARTMENT
THE BRUMBACK LIBRARY
OF VAN WERT COUNTY
VAN WERT, OHIO

GAYLORD

RHINOCEROS BEETLE TO THE RESCUE

Linda Hartley

Photographs by Hidekazu Kubo
GEC Garrett Educational Corporation

The sun shines brightly.

Sounds of insects fill the air.

A new sound is heard at sunset.

Rustle, rustle.

What is that?

It's a black rhinoceros beetle!

W-h-i-r-r-r-r.

The hungry rhinoceros beetle flies away to find food.

The sweet smell

of tree sap fills the air.

Where is it coming from?

The rhinoceros beetle searches.

What's this?

It's a stag beetle with large jaws.

This big beetle doesn't want other insects around.

The rhinoceros beetle nears the stag beetle.

The rhinoceros beetle uses its big jaws to toss little insects away.

The rhinoceros beetle and the stag beetle fight.

Which will win?

Look!

The rhinoceros beetle flips the stag beetle into the air.

The stag beetle

is gone.

Night comes.

Insects return

to share

the tree sap.

The sun rises.

The rhinoceros beetle rests until sunset.

The tree sap still runs.

Insects stop

to enjoy a sweet meal.

Edited by Eril Hughes
Text (c) 1996 by Garrett Educational Corporation
First Published in the United States in 1996 by Garrett Educational Corporation,
130 East 13th Street, Ada, Oklahoma 74820
Copyright 1987 Kaisei-Sha Publishing Co.
All rights reserved including the right of reproduction in whole or in
part in any form
without the prior written permission of the publisher.
Manufactured in the United States of America

Hartley, Linda.
  Rhinoceros beetle to the rescue/ Linda Hartley; Photographs by Hidekazu Kubo.
       p. cm. – (Shining nature)
  Photographs originally published in: Ganbare kabutomushi:/ Kubo Hidekazu shashin. Tokyo : Kaiseisha. 1988. in series:
Shizen kira kira.
  Summary: Photographs and brief text depict a rhinoceros beetle's fight to protect its food. ISBN 1-56074-065-5
  1. Rhinoceros beetle–Juvenile literature. [1. Rhinoceros beetle. 2. Beetles.] I. Kubo. Hidekazu. II. Kubo. Hidekazu.
Ganbare kabutomushi. Selections. III. Title. IV. Series: Hartley, Linda. Shining nature.
QL596.S3H27 1996   595.76'49–dc20   96-27085   CIP   AC